Captai

and the Treasure

Jill Bever and Sheilah Currie

Captain Foot found some old boots that were his grandfather's. Inside one of the boots was a map.

"The treasure is on this island!" shouted Captain Foot. "My grandfather's map shows where to find the buried treasure! Ahoy, maties! Let's go!"

Captain Foot went to the island with his pirates, Long John and Corky, and a boy named Smarty.

The captain gave orders to Long John. "Take seven steps across the sand. Then turn right at the tree and take four steps."

"Follow the stream for ten steps," said Captain Foot. "Then walk five steps toward the waterfall."

Corky dug a deep hole, but there was no treasure.

Then Captain Foot ordered Corky to try to find the treasure. Corky walked seven steps across the sand. He turned right and took four steps. Then he took ten steps along the stream.

"Now take five steps toward the waterfall," shouted the captain. **"Five! No more!"**

"Aaargh!" yelled the captain.

"Where's the treasure?

I read the map very carefully."

"We took just the right number
of steps," said the pirates.

"Then what's the problem?"
shouted the captain.

The pirates shrugged.

The next morning Smarty was looking at the map. He shouted, "Captain! Your grandfather left a clue! Look! It says—

'Follow MY steps to find the treasure. That's the way you have to measure!'

Captain, you have to take the steps,' said Smarty. "The other pirates have longer legs, so they take longer step

Smarty was right. The other pirates had long legs, but the captain's legs were exactly the same length as his grandfather's. Captain Foot took the right number of steps and found the treasure.

Everyone jumped for joy and shouted, **"Treasure!"**